The Risk Taker

Layers and Lessons of Excellence

Charles B. Johnson

The Risk Taker

© 2018 Charles B. Johnson

All rights reserved. No portion of this book may be reproduced, stored in any retrieval system, transmitted in any form, by any means, electronic, photocopying, scanning, or other except for attributed quotations, without prior written permission from the author.

Printed in the United States of America.

Preface

Everyone has been in a situation that they needed to get out of. Whether it was a toxic relationship, poor living environment or just being broke. At what point do you decide to change your situation.? The answer to that last question was simple for me. Inspired to beat all odds against me, I became a risk taker. Those risk made me an artist, author, engineer and finally an entrepreneur. I have learned in order to be successful you have to be willing to take risk. What risk are you willing to take.?

The Risk Taker

About the Author

Humble beginnings grew up in Brownsville Brooklyn the projects, graduated Master Degree in Business Administration. Bachelors in Information technology Cisco Certified Network Engineer (CCNP). Hip Hop Artist aka(bless metaphor). Songwriter. New profound Author, Entrepreneur, Hustler, Millionaire mindset, Real Estate Investor and visionary opportunist.

Email charles1121239@gmail.com

https://www.linkedin.com/in/charles-johnson-57837179/

https://twitter.com/blessmetaphor

The Risk Taker

Dedication

I was inspired to write this book from the heart, in my spirit to give my testimony to my family, friends, my grandmother up in heaven, my music friends, engineer friends business friends, people I grew up with in Brooklyn people that know me from different episodes of my life. I did it for me and to fulfill a bucket list of achieving my goals no matter the hardship the weather, living your fullest potential matters more, than being content with where you are in life. I hope the universe and he who listens transpire to this book and become their greatest self.

The Risk Taker, layers and lessons of excellence
How he came from Brownsville Brooklyn, mindset shift to a winners mentality
"A game Plan to win no matter the weather."

From Artist, to Author to Engineer to Entrepreneur

Table of Contents

Preface ii
About the Author iii
Dedication iv
Chapter 1 Ignorance 1
Chapter 2 The awakening 4
Chapter 3 Failure is not an option 7
Chapter 4 Manifest your reality 9
Chapter 5 Information to Transformation 11
Chapter 6 Winners mentality 12
Chapter 7 Procrastination 14
Chapter 8 Prayer, god and the universe 16
Chapter 9 Inspiration 18
Chapter 10 My personal life 20
Chapter 11 Options to Create a lifestyle on your terms 22
Chapter 12 Research 24
Chapter 13 Adversity, failure, the will to go push forward. 25
Chapter 14 Reinvention of your self 27
Chapter 15 Closure, becoming a goat (greatest of all time) 28

The Risk Taker

Chapter 1

Ignorance

I came from nothing Brooklyn kid from Brownsville projects, had a dream to be a hiphop rap star when I was younger, got into an early relationship for over a decade and life shifted for me. Grandmother raised me, my mother ran the streets never knew who my father was between two men and I came from a drug intoxicated family. College and attending school was not a big thing of importance my family, I had to be self-motivated to finish.my grandmother did all she could to motivate me by paying for me to go away to business school from the projects. I had many dreams but I was ignorant but very inquisitive and took a lot of risk to get ahead. I did a lot of wrong in the neighborhood but writed my wrongs as I got older. I realized if you want to get blessed you must help other people for the right reasons.

I was infatuated with conning people when I was younger, I was a hustler back then and still am till this day except more professional cleaned up. My

The Risk Taker

grandmother Gertie johnson has prepared me for the life I never knew that came before me. Now that she is gone I cherish her words (god don't drill in unclean places} screaming at me to clean my room, telling me about church staying positive in the midst of uncertainty. I always was optimistic and had this fearless mentality to thrive and try new things. I wasn't afraid to fail because I felt in my heart, to live around it in my neighborhood all my life from drug dealers to watching people I know spend their life standing on the corner looking them in their face and seeing them lose hope in their dreams made me realize, my hustle and my plans must change in order to live a lifestyle i always see on the music videos and movie screens. I know what its like to make 7 dollars an hour to making 75$ and more all with mindset.

    This book I decided to write it for many reasons, My Style of writing this book is quite unorthodox, I may not reference everything I am giving you in order please be patient with my story. To continue I wrote this book not for money but to inspire other black men and women out there, that feel like they are hopeless and their dreams can't come true, I am hear to tell you, it can, coming from Brownsville Brooklyn actually made me first a survivor with a hustlers mentality too now a thriver, well off mentality. All this by shifting your mindset, establishing a new circle of friends, investing in yourself, prayer, challenging yourself creating new habits, being held accountable for your actions.

The Risk Taker

I never thought pass the age of 19 yrs old all I wanted to do was make music, have sex with women and finish school or miraculously get rich and live my life on a fantasy. Well the real world kicked in. I can honestly say I am not ashamed of coming from poverty to becoming a mentor to many and transforming to a multimillionaire. This transformation didn't happen over night it took some pain and pressure.

Chapter 2

The awakening

All I knew growing up was to make music write dope lyrics and hopefully shop my tracks to the right people and I would have been a hip star, unfortunately, god had another plan for me, till this day I still feel like I need to at least put out one album which I am to get it out of my system, even though I have evolved to a businessman of many ventures that is taking place before me. How do you become stable in an unstable environment? you tend to think having a degree a certification gets you further in life unfortunately after a matter of time you get wise and you begin to play the game to win, in a world of instant gratification and everything requires a dollar to get ahead.

I gotta be honest with you, this is my first time out, writing a full blown book about my life story and the man I became to be today, but for a moment, let me take you back in time, then bring you back up to speed of where I am today.

The Risk Taker

I was in a relationship with a woman I loved for 14 yrs from age 19 up until the age 33, my life drastically changed for the better but at that time in my life I felt it was the worst experience no man should experience in divorce, but it actually freed me to become the guy I am today. The feeling of losing was already in my neighborhood, my family so, to already lose my mother dying of drugs, not knowing who my father is and last but not least my ex-wife walking out on me has made my views of women quite different. Overall my upbringing as a black man in society made me analyze more why things result in failure activities.

Looking around my environment as a kid I always knew something was wrong in society but I could not pinpoint it. I went to college to occupy my time to get away from the neighborhood to stay productive. But to be honest with you, my college degree didn't propel me to where I am today. I believe it was god, my ambition and taking risk in believing in myself when nobody else would.

It all starts with you, people won't buy into the vision if you don't have a plan in place or has taken some actions steps in achieving some form of success. I am glad I came from Brownsville Brooklyn because it made me the sharp engineer/author/businessman I am today. Sometimes we have to go through rough patches to make diamonds out of us especially blackmen.

The Risk Taker

    I wanted to express myself in this book purely the mere truth of how I feel from poverty to prosperity from the lens of a black American man from the projects with very little guidance with so many trials and errors I have experienced from the job market to learning the political landscape to evolving to an entrepreneur creating my own lane of opportunity when the odds have been stacked against me.

Chapter 3
Failure is not an option

When you don't have a cushion of a backup plan to win and after losing my long-lost love and having to realize, I am out here in the world all alone. My grandmother ain't here no more, my mother is gone and having family sporadically spread out from state to state with random calls through out the year of "(how you doing or what's up cuz) makes me think to myself, the world is colder even if your own family can't help you or don't have a connection someone I know can help me out if I fall. I had to grow up quick coming from the projects friends I went to school with played skelly, blacktime and skated with died or went to jail. When you get older you always want to hear success stories especially where u from. Unfortunately, that was not my story.

So I moved and lived in Newark NJ for some time until moving and obtaining my first multifamily, which changed my financial future. Life has a way of giving you signs when to make decisions in your

The Risk Taker

life that can alter your lifestyle. I decided to educate myself more study, finance, engineering, tax law, self-help books if I were to compete in a society that doesn't value a blackman success like other cultures, in terms of becoming an engineer a successful business man without the stero types associated.

My thoughts of this book is random of me telling you my output of the margin of success is less for blackmen and the ways to catapult your way to success means do what works for you, and not what someone else see's for you. A person will always give you less than what you give yourself in terms of value.

When there is no cushion failure is not an option especially when you have no support and the odds are stacked against you, only way to win is game plan, study research prayer and implement these actions in your life to see changes.

The Risk Taker

Chapter 4

Manifest your reality

Everything I worked on behind the scenes from the age of 16teen doing pushups in my room study for a math test after my black math teacher left the school and I had another teacher that showed no care if I passed to graduate highschool, was the manifest of my life story today. I immediately bought a math book studied even though I was not confident of the regents exam went by faith and doing the hard work to study propelled me to pass a test I didn't care for one bit.

A light bulb went off in my head and made me approach every life challenge I've encountered till this day as a intelligent individual. It's called "strategy". You can win any battle in life if you understand your situation, write it down on paper or a white board list your problems and list solutions or how to tackle your problems one by one. Ninety percent of all our problems is psychological, once we write it out speak of it and implement solutions it becomes easier to deal with our challenges.

The Risk Taker

I recommend you get a vision board and put pictures of where u see your self and your whiteboard should have a to do list on top of all of this you need a mentor to hold you accountable of accomplishing our goals. I know life gets in the way but even myself needs this, trust me without this my manifest of my success would not have transpired without it and of course prayer as a major ingredient to your success rate.

Chapter 5

Information to Transformation

From artist to engineer to author to entrepreneur, I look at things from a different eye of the lens, I was a con artist before being a mature human being and I made a lot of mistakes intentionally and unintentional before realizing there is a pattern for successful habits and a unsuccessful habits. You can only grow when you learn similar to failing you don't fail you learn another lesson, our thoughts dictate our words and our words act out our actions its fact. I say its so important to guard what you watch and listen to everyday because what you filter in your brain lives out in your life whether you want to accept it or not thoughts become things and takes on a transformation of something.

The Risk Taker

Chapter 6

Winners mentality

Whenever I felt pain living in the projects my mother doing drugs, to not knowing who my father is to feeling hopeless I always prayed got on my kness at night, wrote down my problems and brainstorm about a solution to solve my troubles. When the morning came I had a game plan to figure out how can I overcome this issue, no matter if it was money, passing an exam, getting a job I somehow sketched out a game plan on paper. Whenever I felt obstacles were a mountain over my head, I would write out ways to defeat my issue, and after I finish writing my mountain of problems has been reduced to a pebble a strategy to overcome this fear of failure defeatist mentality. ("A winner is someone who took loses and utilize his pain, fear and loss as a solution to seeing some light at the end of the tunnel to win despite the odds life has thrown at him.")

The transition from street project mentality to corporate culture professionalism to Entreprenuer

The Risk Taker

requires a risk taker approach to not taken anyone or anything for granted to win at this game of life.

    By far no means, I am not perfect we all make mistakes and I learned a great deal from my own, your follow through must be consistent to have a winners mentality which leads up to discipline. I know its hard to do even for me at times but overall if you think about the things you want to achieve and begin to plant seeds of action your harvest grows when you speak it, think it do it and perform it.

The Risk Taker

Chapter 7

Procrastination

Being an network engineer has its perks but also has it down fall, the transition into career mode as been a rocky climb for me, but I do appreciate it, me sticking through the rough patches to become a network engineer, I procrastinated a lot on my studies in which I still feel like I don't know enough of the field that I am in, even though technology is constantly changing and I am in a field where you must keep learning to become a valuable asset to yourself and aka the company you work for. I love what I do but on the flipside I love my time more as an entrepreneur. The challenge of an engineer requires discipline and consistency of training. I like to be challenged but I also like to live a certain lifestyle. The moral of the story is master your learning style so you can absorb knowledge and move on to the next skillset, one of my gifts as an engineer is I have the ability to learn it quick and incorporate the new skill into my learning style, (Always do what works for you). Like

The Risk Taker

I said before everything you need to achieve begins with a thought stop procrastinating and write it down post on your whiteboard look at it everyday or type it in your smartphone as a reminder, this way your killing procrastination and you have a goal haunting you until you get it done. So get it done.

The Risk Taker

Chapter 8

Prayer, god and the universe

I tell you as a blackman from poverty and my mother naming me my middle name (Bless) I swear from the heavens up above and hearing my grandmothers voice, when I look back from once I came. I swear I am blessed. All of my prayers have come true not the way I perceived but because I am not going to church everyday kinda guy but I do believe in god, There were times of being alone and I felt unsure of my circumstances god doesn't lie and karma comes around good or bad. Sometimes when you pray and speak those words of affirmation you be surprised 10 days or a year later you begin to realize what you been asking for has been forming into your life. Be careful and confident of what you ask the universe because it does come true. I am a believer in miracles and spiritual fate of things happening for a reason, this part of my life grew more after the lost of my mother, grandmother and ex wife leaving my life as a man to carry on I truly understand the meaning of love

The Risk Taker

and feeling the lost of hope, and when your love ones depart out of your control but everything is meant to happen for a reason. All I can do as is grow from these experiences it's inevitable change is inevitable.

I do pray for my family and everyone that had ever had an impact on my life as well. I never planned for this part of my life but I appreciate the trial and tribulations that has led me down this path of greatness. I believe the universe has a way of rebalancing your life by the impact you have on others. You make a stain or make a mark in life which one are you.

Chapter 9
Inspiration

The impact you have on people is equally important to your momentum, without struggle you can't appreciate the good and the bad, sometimes we need inspiration to motivate us out of the deepest darkest moments in our lives times of need be the times of great growth and change spiritual shifting takes place and the rebirth of a person has been changed forever. All this has happened to me from telling myself I'm better than this job my worth is more than this the mental talking to myself and feeding my brain successful images of blackmen black entrepreneur does something to the subconscious mind. What you feed yourself information wise has a big impact on your growth as a professional. Iron sharpens iron, it pays well to be around someone or in a group to be inspired. The key to staying inspired is momentum when in the groove don't stop. I say this because when you look back at your achievements, those timeless moments propel you to the next

The Risk Taker

achievement ahead, it's soft of like your Michael Jordan or LeBron or Mayweather winning the championship title. You broke barriers and that feeling of being a winner against the grain all odds is impeccable and sometimes words cant express that feeling of joy of accomplishment. All of this sums up to a winners mentality.

The Risk Taker

Chapter 10
My personal life

Growing up in Brooklyn Brownsville projects has made me a proud blackman despite all odds. I am glad I have overcome the statistic views of white America, I can honestly say I am comfortable being who I am as blackman and not having the support system to some degree has held me back but in some cases made me propel forward in my career, dreams, aspirations of what I became today. Thoughts become things and growing up around drug dealers, thieves and crackheads sure made me grow up quick when everything around me was not to the betterment of my quality of life to win but to lose and stay in a trap. I like to give credit to my grandmother Gertie Johnson and Sharlene Johnson my mother and my grandmother for raising me and bringing me into the world when the deck always has been stacked against me and still is but I appreciate the challenge my grandmother was a hussler she has taught me to this day to go out there get yours keep a dollar in your

The Risk Taker

wallet and "god don't drill in unclean places") she use to say to me, when I never cleaned my room.(lol) Now I appreciate all of her nagging screaming at me when she was alive. Out of all of this being around my uncles and older grandfather figures has made me and ol' soul of what you may call it, the transition from Artist to Author to Engineer to Entrepreneur has layers of fascination in my journey. Thank you for taking the time out to read my journey.

The Risk Taker

Chapter 11

Options to Create a lifestyle on your terms

The mindset shift from being ignorant of not knowing how to approach life, being unemployed Year after year I began to recognize a pattern of money flow depleting , pretty much going up and down, like the stock market from having a job to not having a job, I had to figure out a way where you can live a lifestyle without the dependence of a job, at first you must work a job but only treat that money to invest in your dreams and freedom to carving a path of financial independence from investing in real estate, your business, investment clubs, and index funds, bonds and etf's for the long term gain. In the mean time develop multiple side businesses online, create partnerships invest in other people business to create side revenue, teach, become a value to your brand invest in marketing yourself and begin to leverage credit to your advantage. Clean your credit keep it under 30% and most important

The Risk Taker

establish business credit, apply for a business license of your choice LLc's S corp etc.. Having options of not having to work for anyone but exist and live the life of goals being accomplished is the way to go.

To add to the fire, your intentions of writing things down of what you want and desire, will come to reality. I say this because everything I have written down manifested into real life I was shocked it may not have been exact but I started to compare what I written down months ago or a year ago and it was always 90% accurate of what I was looking for. Sometimes you have to ask the universe write it down and pray on it also act on it for it to transform into a real life reality for you try it. These things help you create the lifestyle you want on your terms.

Chapter 12

Research

Research makes the difference between making great choices in your life, this is what I have encountered, reading, studying is a lost art coming from a bad environment allowed me to embrace it and find some good out of my circumstances, which made me dig deeper into my studies and research on life, career, finances and where I see my self in the near future. Brownsville Brooklyn was and is the foundation of my success I have today. The ability to deep dive into a topic or thing is very essential, as we are in the information age it's critical to be on top of your game for whatever profession your good at, if you can take the time and study without distraction then you have a hidden gem of focus that brings your research skills at the top of the food chain.

The Risk Taker

Chapter 13

Adversity, failure, the will to go push forward.

The feeling of feeling invincible, your making six figure salary, money is coming in, making plans for my investments, then suddenly the rug gets pulled from under me, yes the feeling of losing your job because of these petty politics your not good enough, your performance, etc. Now you have to go home tell your family friends, the feeling seeps in, all the plans you made gets put to a halt, you,ve acquired more debt took on additional benefits and life slaps you in the face. This is what happen to me, forever battling the unemployment line year after year, putting my best foot forward. The level of motivation to invest buy a house I was on my way then adversity strikes. This moment of my life alone I my apartment in Newark NJ before my breakthrough I was sad, torn depressed, asking god what did I do wrong ". Then suddenly I had to remain focus, did some soul searching and began to focus again. All of a sudden my life began to encounter opportunites that changed my life forever. I got another gig and I worked it long enough to invest in my property and the rest is history.

    The gut feeling of losing, having a task to complete,feeling hoplessness and needing of a mentor to get over the hump to achive my architect certification was dire to me. In my heart of hearts I had to complete it because I came this far in my journey. Even though my heart was not in it when I first started but somehow I had to complete the journey because I spent, all this money and didn't put in the time so I was under the eightball to produce results for myself and being accountable. God be the glory if it wasn't for good friends like Ahmed, Emmanuel and Gloria I don't know where I would be. I am now a home owner with multifamily properties and my financial troubles are long behind me, my investments ive made paid off for my career and my entrenprenuer risk.. vs reward. Got me to the level I am at with a mix of friends god and the most high.

Chapter 14
Reinvention of your self

The Power to learn and relearn new things can become fun and exhausting at the same time. Especially, when your will power has been tested time and time again, from losing jobs not because your not good enough but the politics, the market white supremacy mix of factors beyond your control. Only thing you can control is your will power to change and bend when adversity strikes in the midst of change for the better. To reinvent yourself is a power attribute against all odds. It's a skill and a wit to have survival mechanism when you must go against the grain. The beauty of it all is adaptability to change when you must grow, this ties into being uncomfortable reinvention requires constant uncomfortabilty trying new things when you don't know, im talking from experience and still I am trying new things to remain open and constant learning life. The results are amazing.

Chapter 15

Closure, becoming a goat (greatest of all time)

I never thought of writing a book about my life and different views or layers of my life. I hope to achieve greatness in the grace of god and inspire someone else reading this book, to take the information and know that, they too can become successful in which I call it, becoming a (GOAT) greatest of all time in your profession, the person you are that makes you, unique stand out be comfortable in your skin, creative and personal expression is healthy. As for me not knowing who my father is growing up in Brownsville and from experiencing the pain of people walking out of my life, I always wanted closure for answers that never came. Because of this feeling of emptiness inside I took this pain of hurt and painted this book of expression and with my music as well. I say this to say to all that is reading this book thank you for taking the time to get to know me on a personal level and professional level as well, in order to be

The Risk Taker

great you must be afraid to fail and keep moving forward in life despite your outcomes. This book is my closure to say I am Artist, Author, Entreprenuer Engineer Multimillionaire, investor, philanthropist future father, husband gods son black man achiever everything you can become starts with you and your mind peace be still amen.

www.ingramcontent.com/pod-product-compliance
Lightning Source LLC
Chambersburg PA
CBHW071550080526
44588CB00011B/1856